GUID

GIRLFRIEND

A Personalized Map for Your Boyfriend

MAKENZIE HAGESTAD

Brown Books Publishing Group

Dallas, Texas

Guide to Your Girlfriend
A Personalized Map for Your Boyfriend

Brown Books Publishing Group
16250 Knoll Trail Drive, Suite 205
Dallas, Texas 75248
www.BrownBooks.com
(972) 381-0009

A New Era in Publishing™

ISBN 978-1-61254-135-8
LCCN 2013947401

Printed in the United States
10 9 8 7 6 5 4 3 2 1

For more information or to contact the author, please go to www.GuideToYourGirlfriend.com

This book is dedicated to the good friend and man who inspired it. There would be no book if it wasn't for you.

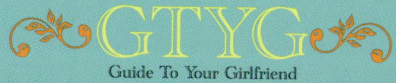

Photo Here

Contents

Acknowledgments

I would like to express sincere gratitude to the following:

My family and friends who have helped me through the entire book creation process. By letting me run ideas by you, giving your opinion on cover designs, and even assisting with editing multiple versions, your insights and support have meant the world to me.

Milli and the entire Brown Books Publishing team, for enabling my dream to become a reality.

My Kappa Alpha Theta sisters for supporting my idea from the get-go and always being my go-to focus group.

Last, but certainly not least, my mother for recognizing that what was originally a crafty gift I made for a boyfriend could in fact be a book that would help other young couples better understand and communicate with one another. And for being brave enough to form a company with a twenty-year-old in order to work together and achieve our dreams.

Dear Girlfriends,

Think of this book as a way to help you help yourself. This is for all those times you may become frustrated or upset with your guy over the smallest—or biggest—of things. From important dates to your favorite flowers, everything he needs to know is in here.

Guys operate differently than we do. For example, most of the time we know our man's favorite everything, whereas he probably doesn't know ours. We know they care; sometimes they just focus on different things than you do. So think of this book as a way for you to lend your boyfriend a hand before he even knows he needs one.

Dear Boyfriends,

This book is a thoughtful gift made specifically for you. We all know that men and women think differently. When the two of you don't see eye-to-eye, frustration and stress can take their toll on your relationship. You could know your girlfriend is upset, but you may not know why or what you can do to fix it. Or maybe you want to plan the perfect outing and could use a few pointers.

Enclosed in this book are answers, tips, and step-by-step instructions on how to avoid pitfalls and how to surprise her in the very best of ways.

Think of this book as a cheat sheet or playbook of sorts. When a situation arises and you aren't sure what to do, you can look to the Guide to navigate your way through.

Photo Here

Chapter 1
Moods

Navigating the Highs, Lows,
and Everything In-Between

Aggravated

Definition

Symptoms

Sayings to watch for

Cure

Anxious

Definition

Symptoms

Sayings to watch for

Cure

Bored

Definition

Symptoms

Sayings to watch for

Cure

Excited

Definition

Symptoms

Sayings to watch for

Cure

Frustrated

Definition

Symptoms

Sayings to watch for

Cure

Happy

Definition

Symptoms

Sayings to watch for

Cure

Hungry

Definition

Symptoms

Sayings to watch for

Cure

Moody

Definition

Symptoms

Sayings to watch for

Cure

Sad

Definition

Symptoms

Sayings to watch for

Cure

Sick

Definition

Symptoms

Sayings to watch for

Cure

Stressed

Definition

Symptoms

Sayings to watch for

Cure

Tired

Definition

Symptoms

Sayings to watch for

Cure

Definition

Symptoms

Sayings to watch for

Cure

Definition

Symptoms

Sayings to watch for

Cure

_ _ _ _ _ _ _ _ _ _ _ _ _ _ _ _

Definition

Symptoms

Sayings to watch for

Cure

_ _ _ _ _ _ _ _ _ _ _ _ _ _ _

Definition

Symptoms

Sayings to watch for

Cure

Photo Here

Chapter 2
Communication
Sometimes We Speak Two Different Languages

how to read me

over text

Fine

What I Say

What I Mean

What I Say

Whatever

What I Mean

What I Say

What I Mean

What I Say

What I Mean

What I Say

What I Mean

What I Say

What I Mean

Contacts

Name

Relation

Phone Number

E-mail

Name

Relation

Phone Number

E-mail

Name

Relation

Phone Number

E-mail

Name

Relation

Phone Number

E-mail

Name

Relation

Phone Number

E-mail

Name

Relation

Phone Number

E-mail

Name

Relation

Phone Number

E-mail

Caring Expressions

We all need something special.
It really shows me that you care when...

You tell me...

You show me...

You surprise me with...

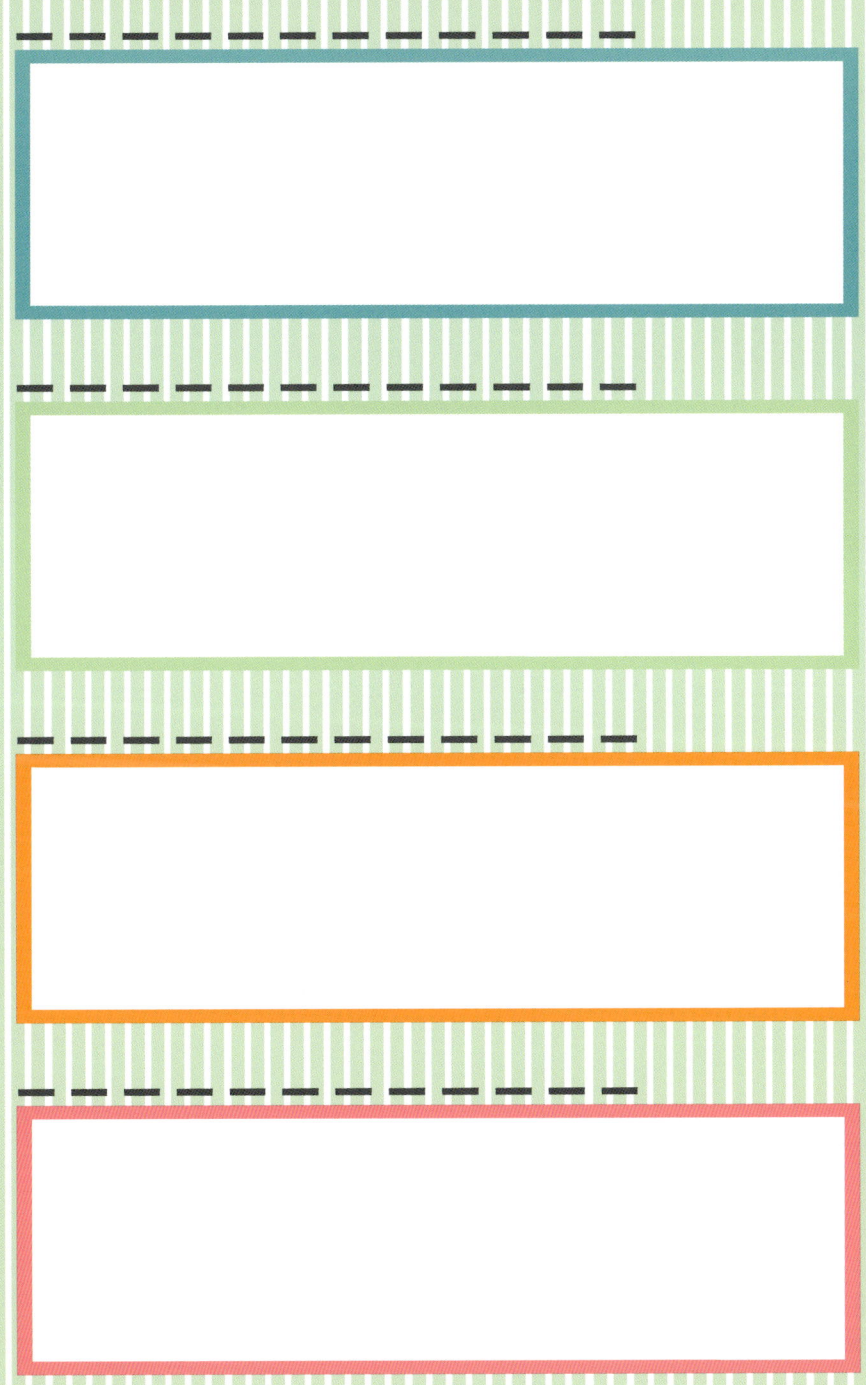

Photo Here

Chapter 3
Favorite Things
Ways You Can Never Go Wrong

Favorite Foods

Entrée

Sides

Dessert

Food When I'm Sick

Candy

Comfort Foods

Soda

Ice Cream

Other Drinks

Snacks

Entertainment

Movies

Favorite Movie of All Time

Scary

Chick Flick

Action

Sad

TV Shows

Music

Favorite Song of All Time

Genres

Musical Groups

Basics

Animal   Flowers

Color

Favorite Place in the Entire World

Perfume

Holiday

Activities

Hobbies

College Sports

Pro Sports Team

Sports I Play

Sports I Watch

All About You

My Favorite Things About You

My Favorite Moments With You

My Heart Melts When . . .

Photo Here

Chapter 4
Date Ideas

Star Gazing

What to Bring

When to Do This

Movie Marathon

What to Bring

When to Do This

Picnic

What to Bring

When to Do This

Watching Sunrise/Sunset

What to Bring

When to Do This

Drive-In Movie

What to Bring

When to Do This

Make a Meal Together

What to Bring

When to Do This

Game Night

What to Bring

When to Do This

Local Attractions
(Zoo, Water Park, Amusement Park, Museum)

What to Bring

When to Do This

Couples Dance Class

What to Bring

When to Do This

What to Bring

When to Do This

----- ----- ----- ----- ----- ----- ----- -----

What to Bring

When to Do This

----- ----- ----- ----- ----- ----- -----

What to Bring

When to Do This

Photo Here

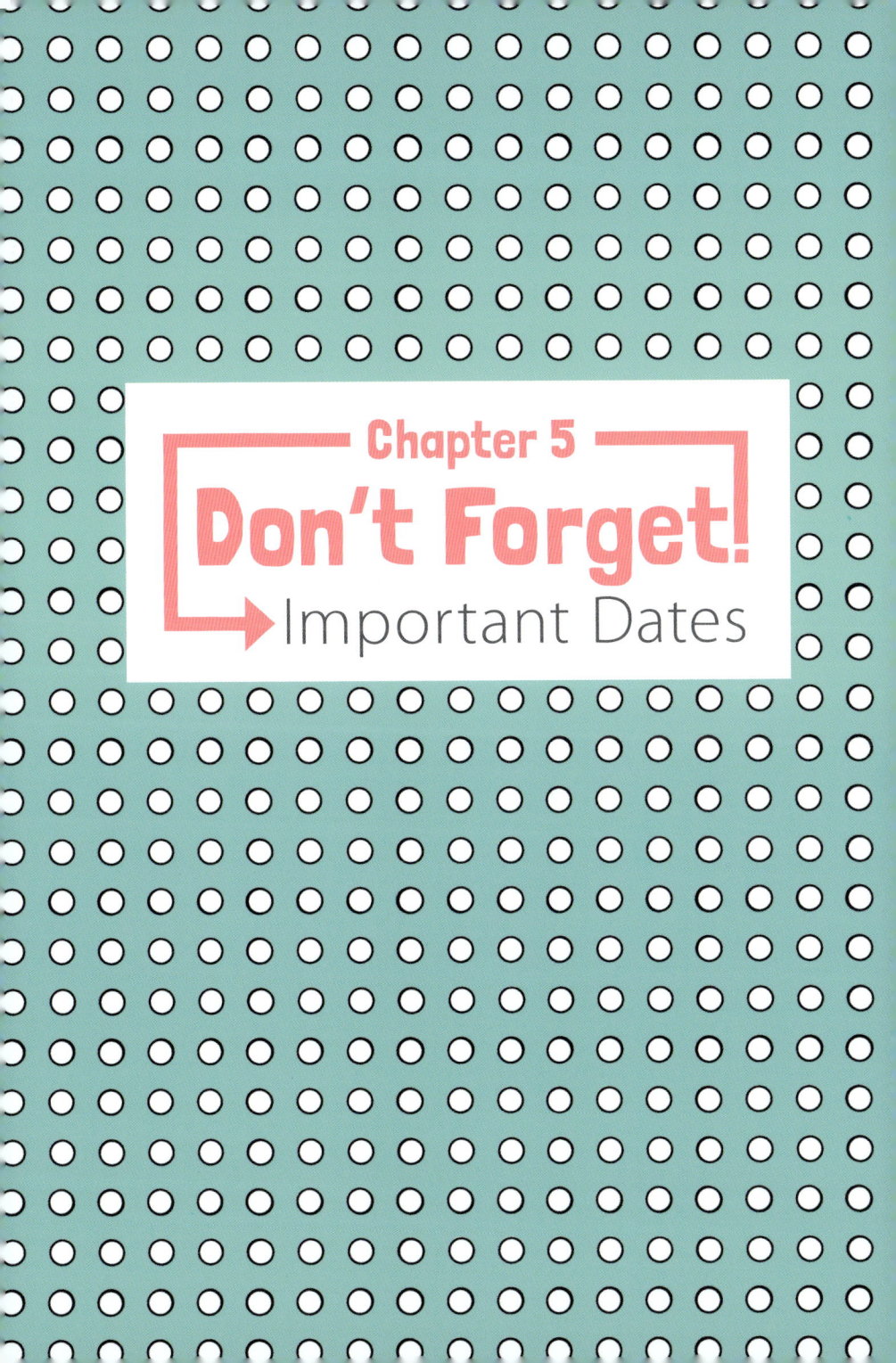

Chapter 5

Don't Forget!

→ Important Dates

January

February

March

April

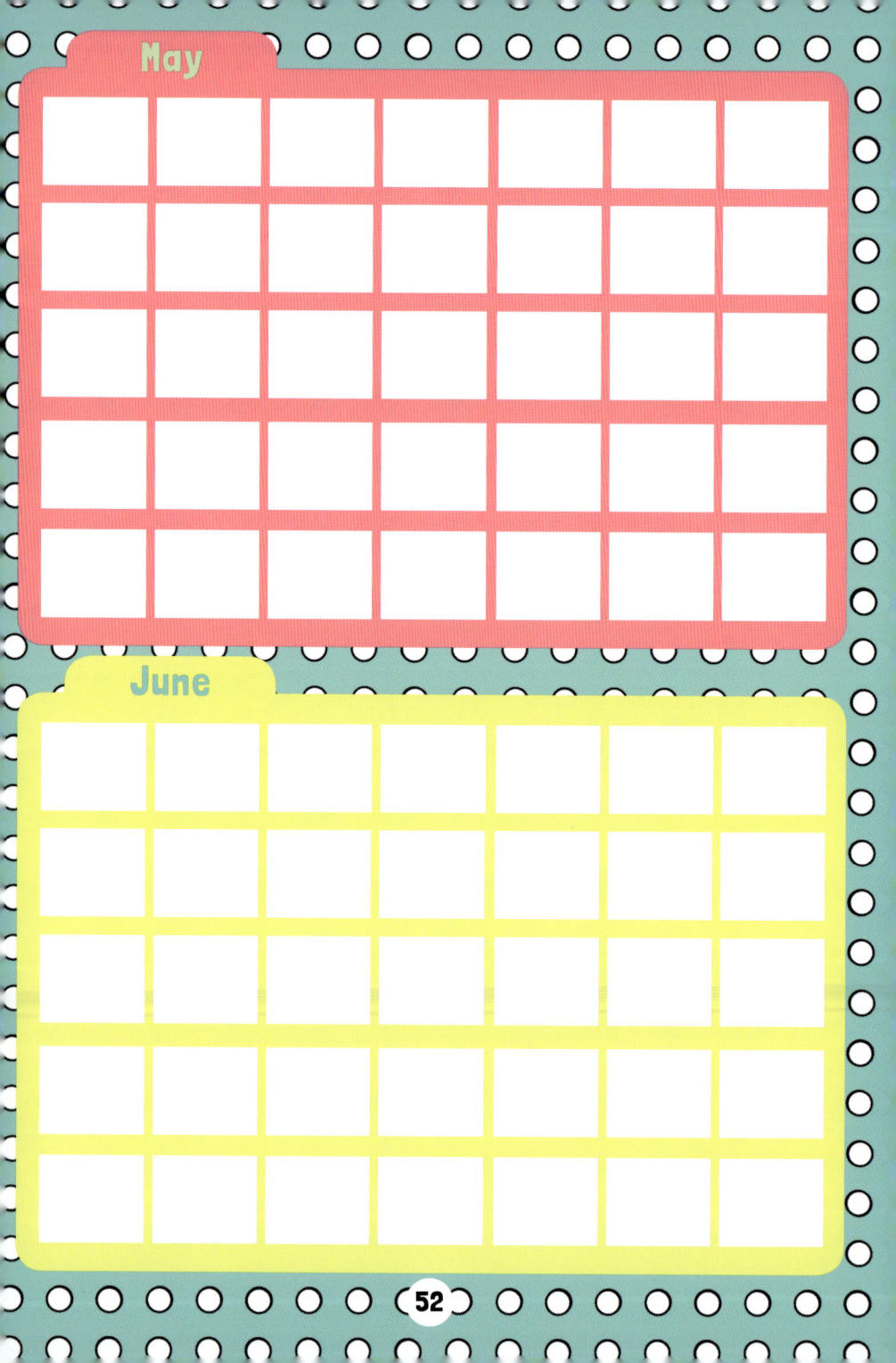

May

June

July

August

September

October

November

December

Photo Here

Chapter 6
Fill Me In

About The Author

MAKENZIE HAGESTAD wants to help couples straighten out the crossed lines of communication between them. Throughout her life, Makenzie saw countless instances of miscommunication between her and the men in her life. She thought surely there was a clever way to facilitate basic communication between the sexes.

The eureka moment came in 2012 when her then-boyfriend continuously found himself in the dog house! In an attempt to help him, she created a blueprint to her heart—a handmade booklet to be used as a tool to decipher the miscommunication between them and spark some romance in the process. Come to find out, it worked! The next year, Makenzie leveraged her creativity, sass, and street smarts to write *Guide to Your Girlfriend*. This personalized "playbook" provides your guy with all the inside information he'll need to be the perfect boyfriend.

Sorority girl and Baylor University fashion merchandising major, Makenzie already has another creative idea up her sleeve. It's hush-hush for now but could very well be the next Guide book to . . . ?